Unbelievable Pictures and Facts About Romania

By: Olivia Greenwood

12.99

Introduction

Romania is a very unique country which is situated in Europe. Here you will find many churches, castles, old buildings, and towers. We will be learning all sorts of interesting and fun facts about Romania.

Do many people come to visit Romania?

Over the years Romania has become a much more popular country to visit than it was in the past. Many people from different parts of the world come to visit Romania.

Will you find any waterfalls in Romania?

There are many wonderful waterfalls for you to see all over the country.

Did any fictional characters originate from Romania?

Dracula is a vampire character that was created in Romania. It is based on a real person who was born in Transylvania.

What kinds of food do people eat in Romania?

People eat all sorts of food in the country. Some of the popular dishes include meat and cabbage and smoked bacon with rice.

Which religion is practiced the most in the country?

The religion which is practiced the most in the country is Christianity.

Does the country have a national flower?

The country does have a national flower. The name of this national flower is the dog rose.

On average how long do people in the country live for?

The people in Romania have a tendency to live very long lives. Women live up until 80 years of age and men live up until 75 years of age.

What kind of landscape is there in Romania?

Romania has a very scenic type of landscape. The country is surrounded by springs, lakes, mountains and beautiful hills.

Are there any castles in Romania?

There are many castles situated all over Romania. If you ever wanted to visit a real castle, then you will be glad to know that Romania can make those dreams come true.

What goods do they export from the country?

They export many different goods from the country. Some of the most popular goods which they export are cars, wheat, wine, and food products.

What languages do people speak in Romania?

The main language which they speak in Romania is Romanian. Many people consider this to be a language of love.

What financial currency do they use in Romania?

If you plan on buying anything in the country, you will need to know what currency they use. The financial currency which they use in Romania is the Romanian Leu.

Are there any rivers in Romania?

You will find plenty of rivers running all through the country of Romania.

Where will you find the tallest point in the country?

If you are looking for the tallest point in the country will you find it at a place called Moldoveanu.

Are there any animals in Romania?

Romania is filled with all sorts of animals. There are over 33,792 different animal species currently living in Romania.

What type of weather is there in Romania?

Romania is known for its bitterly cold winters. It gets freezing cold during the winter times. During the summer months, the sun shines and the weather has a tendency to become a bit warmer.

Is the cost of living high in Romania?

It depends on the part of Romania that you wish to stay. It also depends on the type of lifestyle which you want to live in. Although on average the cost of living in Romania is not too high. It is actually lower in comparison to many other places.

It is safe to travel in Romania?

It is actually very safe to travel in Romania. However, you need to always be careful when you travel regardless of where you go.

Which city in Romania is the capital?

The name of the capital of Romania is Bucharest.

Where in the world will you find Romania?

Far away on the continent of Europe, you will find Romania. It lies very close to the Southeastern side of Central Europe.

Made in the USA
Monee, IL
16 August 2020